#Hypocrisy
Imogen Stirling

Speculative Books
Glasgow
All Rights Reserved
© Copyright 2019
ISBN: 978-1-912917-05-1
Words by Imogen Stirling
Cover & illustrations by Sean Mulvenna
www.speculativebooks.net

"#Hypocrisy is a tonic for the tribal times we live in. Even the most right-on among us can be ignorant twats sometimes. It's encouraging to see this explored in depth, within the uber-progressive context of spoken word. Stirling does it effortlessly, with humour, self-awareness and grace."

Darren 'Loki' McGarvey

"Imogen Stirling goes through the painstaking task of deconstructing her own whiteness and privilege, and does so in a way that is inviting, profound, humorous and unsettling. #Hypocrisy is exactly the sort of poetry we need right now, in these dark and difficult times."

Alan Bissett

Preview performances:
Latitude Festival, Eden Festival,
Dram! Glasgow (all summer 2018)

Debut performance:
#Hypocrisy debuted at the Edinburgh Fringe 2018 at the Scottish Poetry Library. The show sold out its run and was long listed for the Amnesty International Freedom of Expression Award.

Subsequent performances:
#Hypocrisy transferred to London's Theatre503 as part of their 'Best of the Fest' programme.

Future performances:
#Hypocrisy began its 2019 UK tour at Traverse Theatre (Edinburgh) and CCA (Glasgow).

The show is touring mainland Europe before showcasing at Prague Fringe Festival 2019 and running at Alphabetti Theatre, Newcastle.

Ross Somerville (composer/guitarist)

Ross Somerville has been composing music for shows since 2011. Graduating in Film and TV/Theatre Studies from Glasgow University with a Masters degree in Film, he has composed for six Edinburgh Fringe shows, including Lace Up (Trig Point Theatre/New Celts ****), Erin, Errol and the Earth Creatures (Modest Predicament ****). Ross' music centres around ambient textures with driving melodies, inspired by the likes of John Hopkins, Bonobo, Mogwai and Final Fantasy series' composer Nobuo Uematsu.

Finnie Welsh (percussionist)

Finnie Welsh is a multi-instrumentalist living in Glasgow and the newest addition to the #Hypocrisy team. He has been performing in different bands ranging from folk to hip hop as well as theatrical productions for a number of years and has spent much of his upbringing in the arts and playing music.

Imogen Stirling (writer/performer)

Imogen Stirling is a performance poet, theatre maker and musician. Her music accolades include an 18 month tour around mainland Europe as one half of duo 'Wonderful Exile', receipt of the Alasdair Cameron Scholarship for her political musical theatre piece, BodiesUponTheGears, and work alongside Sir Tim Rice. An award-winning poetry slam champion, Imogen has performed extensively throughout the UK, including at Latitude Festival, Eden Festival, Audacious Women Festival and the Edinburgh Fringe. Imogen toured the UK with hip hop poetry collective Words w/ Friends in summer 2018 before debuting her solo show #Hypocrisy at the Edinburgh Fringe. The show sold out its run and was long listed for the Amnesty International Freedom of Expression Award. It transferred to London's Theatre503 as part of their 'Best of the Fest' programme where it received a five star review. #Hypocrisy is currently touring the UK (covered by BBC Scotland) and mainland Europe, and will be showcasing at the Prague Fringe Festival 2019. Imogen also works as Project Officer for ground-breaking independent publisher, 404 Ink.

This script was written to be read aloud

Part One

WHITE

Eggshell, ghost, pure, Dutch
Such a range of ways to grade this shade
Called
White
Fun fact
I am white
You could say
Very white
For originally red haired
My skin is fairer than most, and
Hailing from Scotland
That pasty wee neighbour of
Lauded Great Britain
I wear this Celtic curse of pale
Meanwhile, in a style unashamedly Western
My veins ebb too with American blood
Thus two superpowers meet here in my body
To form their mix of pale and privilege
Even when basted in sun rays
My skin rarely tans
Instead it stays true to its fairness

As though it can't bear to betray its heritage of
Smallest numbers, biggest egos
Filthy history, cleanest slate though

Even so
I see that I'm lucky
For I have done nothing
For I'm a result of blind birthplace luck that means
I come from this place of white privilege
I speak from this place of white privilege
And so I wrote a show
All about race!

Please don't go, you've already paid

Wait - and give time
To my reliable insight
For you'll find I am well cultured
I am well travelled
For I so unusually
Went backpacking after university

INTERLUDE 1

One and a half years travelling
Busking
Street music performing
My partner and I
Were a musical triumph
Unleashed from our studies
Fresh faced and bright eyed
We kept our silken homespun ties tight round our wrists
For interim bungee distance from home
Yet for that time fully embracing the lone nomad state
We called our band

Wonderful Exile

A name changed mid travel to fulfil
Whimsical fantasies of a new identity
See -
It was all very romantic
Captured in
The tragedy of nomadism
We had ourselves runaways

Outcast from society
Penniless wanderers
Renegade warriors
No home to run to
No one to turn to
Exiled and spurned with
No place to return to

Not entirely true

EXILE

Standing by the side of the road, cold
Fingers turned numb from holding this piece
                            of wind-tattered cardboard
So long; my plans at the mercy of
This handcrafted signage of hope
So kindly asking for transport to Frankfurt, to Paris, Geneva
Or even this time just twenty miles
down the street
for a fresh try
at this

I never liked hitching a lift, it feels degrading
I'd much rather pay the extra for a better way to get there
But it's good to be authentic, I tell myself
Keep it rough, keep it tough, love
The vagabond vibes
Yet my rides keep passing and passing with
Gazes averted, this backpack is hurting my shoulders
I have not eaten for hours
I am in need of a shower
And though it's clear no one's stopping

Cos we've too much to carry
It allows me to wallow in my fantasy of banishment
Put the day down to character enhancement
Exaggerate a sob story adequate to guarantee
A top-performing post on my top-performing blog
It kind of worked out as I wanted

Wonderful Exile
Was a meditated, cover bases name of
Adventure come melancholy
Danger come safety
The vibrant migrant turned Instagram pretty

> *It didn't make me feel discomfort at the time,*
> *too consumed in the glamour of diaspora*

And how I basked in the fantasy of self-imposed exile
Of temporary exile
Of wonderful exile
Of come-home-whenever-you-choose kind of exile
Obviously
The hypocrisy was lost on me

My phone's vibration declares some message from home

A reminder that I am by no means alone, and though
I'm shorter on euros than I'd like to be, the emergency
Credit card awarded by my family
Is guarantee that I will never go hungry
Nor homeless
And though this life on the road
Had its moments of lonesome
There never was a time I did not feel welcome
No, rather than displaced
Every place offered itself as a new abode
For my taking, gifted
Long-term stay in Amsterdam, Berlin, Montpellier
It became an effort to stay away from a home base, so
Cradled in the strong, muscled arms of my passport
I passed through countries
Without a second glance
Borders melted in the distance
Oblivious to privilege – I thought surely
Everyone must live like this

Not entirely true

INTERLUDE 2

There was that one time on the French border when passport control held our bus for almost two hours while the one black passenger was questioned and questioned and questioned in a small sealed room while staff apologised profusely and profusely and profusely and offered the rest of us unlimited coffee and croissants for our trouble. British conformist mindset kicked in, kept us quiet and reminded: it does not pay to be different.

Not entirely true

DIFFERENT

Different sells
Different is sexy
Different is celebrated
Different is business

Different is Scottish not British
Different is vegan not veggie
Different is the sole female busker on a street full of men
Different is the sole ukulele on a street of guitars
Different finds a niche role to keep the pennies rolling
To keep the travel happening
To keep the people buying
Different demands to stand out
It takes every label
It ticks every box
Collects every category and makes itself a blog
Unveiling itself as a
Scottish, female, vegan, digital nomad,
        low-budget travel, voyaging musician
Nobody can match it
And everybody loves it

Different loves to be loved, and
Different knows what is loved, so
Different teases with its passport
Flirts with its accent
Hints at its education
To show it is legitimate
Different
Pairs spontaneity with its stability
Making clear that though different
It still is safe

Because different knows there are limits to difference
Different knows it can only be so different
It keeps quiet when it needs to, speaks up when required to
and overall knows it must only go so far
and just like that-

Different grows hard

Different notices others only to judge them
Has no scruples when it comes to attention
Different prioritises self-preservation
Develops tunnel vision
So different can stay different at expense of all else, and

Different stays on trend
So that different can sell
So that
Different is sexy
Different is celebrated
Different is business
Different is exotic
Different is exciting
Different is enticing
When the right kind of different

INTERLUDE 3

And I was the right kind of different
And I was the good kind of right different
And I was the most kind of good right different

Because I stood out from my peers
This travel was no holiday, no gap year,
         no trust-fund backed exploit
This was Real Life

Months passed, I kept going, kept earning
It was no gift, I worked hard for the way I was living
I deserved it
Because I played music for hours in sweltering heat
         or snow-covered streets
Rehearsed daily unfailingly
I was diligent, I was disciplined
Networked where necessary
Cut back when need be
Moved my way through Europe with no help from nobody

Not entirely true

There was that time I lost my passport but was let on the plane anyway. There was that time I couldn't actually afford a place to stay but turned on the waterworks, offered to play a few songs and I got my way. There was that time my partner had a penknife in his pocket as we crossed into Spain and security turned a blind eye while I watched others be detained. There was that time – nay those many times – I was given gigs over local bands so audiences could watch a 'lovely British girl' on stage and that was the money that paid my way.

Now perhaps they were subtle encouragements
invisible privileges, platform priorities
Unfairly given
But it was to niceness! Not whiteness

I'm aware this reasoning's somewhat flawed
There's a sense of discomfort I can't quite interpret
A discrepancy lingering suggesting unfair division
But what can I do? I didn't ask for it
When I go home there'll be no more need to be different

Not entirely true

HIPSTER

Everybody wants to be a hipster
I come home, different's taken over
And I adore it

The bearded baristas
The hashtag heroes
The craft beer, the matcha
The smashed avocados
The tattoos, the typewriters
Gluten-free dieters
Instagram, Instagram, Instagram
Worshippers

Everybody wants to be a hipster
I come home, different's taken over
Time for my go at breaking this mould

I dye my hair
I get the piercings
Start writing poetry
Learn how to tarot read

Know which wine is which and
Which coffee to ditch and
I think I could get used to living like this

Everybody wants to be the most hipster
I come home different's taken over
And grown addictive
Whose beard is the longest
Whose man bun the tightest
Who's the best read
Knows their Hamlet from Titus
Don't know what the goal is
But we're all chasing it
Topping the craze and the craze and the craze and
It's all competition
Post-modern ambition
It's all a distraction
Isn't it?

Because something is missing amidst it

We inflate the gravity of this dress up game
We engage the safe space to exercise difference
To learn to talk, recite and proffer

But not to offer any real substance
Seems unconstructive, seems over indulgent
Seems underwhelming, seems empty headed
Seems where is the empathy
When we resort to trending hashtags to mitigate apathy
Seems appearance may have superseded moral integrity

INTERLUDE 4

But y'know whatever

There's evident futility in trying to manipulate
        the manner of social conscience
So
If that's how it is then that's how it is
And I am content with how it is
And I don't resent just how it is
And I will get on with how it is

Not entirely true

I mean I like a beard and espresso as much
As the next millenial
But it's all existing in parallel with, well,
Everything else
I'm finding there's a lot of skeletons in my closet as I watch the relics of my travels: the penknives, the passports, the free gigs, the blind eyes build up and up and up and -
See abroad, I could pretend
Life was a bubble

Was trouble free
It was easy to bowl along on privilege,
          play up the ignorance, be the tourist
When I wanted to, needed to
There was enough going on to keep me from the off points
And I could
Switch off from the news, use the excuse of
Foreign papers and limited WiFi
Seeing nothing but blue skies and open seas for me
But now that I'm home
The illusion evaporates
Distractions diminish
And I find that I cannot switch off from this

Part Two

HELEN AND AMAL

Touchdown in Glasgow
I have so missed this city
Famed for our drinks, our rain
And our sense of community
Our motto is People Make Glasgow

Helen and Amal feed the birds in Queens Park every morning
Helen is 80, Amal in her 30s
I see them on my way to work
Helen hands bread to Amal
who ventures down to the water's edge
Sometimes the ducks take it straight
from her hand on a good day
Helen likes to buy wholewheat
but Amal prefers Morrison's morning rolls
When one duck steals another's bread she calls it
Ya wee bastard
Amal has stayed with Helen for the past year
And is treated like the daughter Helen never had
Helen is fiercely protective of Amal's privacy
And respects that

Amal prefers to go out first thing in the morning
Almost before the day wakes

She seems afraid of her Muslim identity

In a world come to see her as enemy

TERROR

In a world that centres on terror

See
I step off the plane and into a world
Of terror
It's on everyone's lips
On every front cover
Perpetrators are taking the places of
A-list tabloid shaming
But while the fear of it dominates
It seems reactions fluctuate
And revised definitions isolate
Cos you'd think
Terror is terror
It's in the name
It's terrifying
Dictionaries describe it as
"violence or the threat of violence"
It is generic
Prevalent and tireless
Terror is terror

Ungendered, uncoloured
Yet
We see its severity
Rendered subjective

To demonstrate

When ISIS hit Paris it was a travesty
Facebook came out with its checkpoints of safety
Friends turned their photos to
Tricolore memory
Yet
Only the day previous
Beirut had experienced its worst hit in decades
Just like Paris, claimed by the same
Each city outsiders
But we grieved with the French and kept
Lebanon silenced

And that's no anomaly

Because we all cried for Nice and not Bangladesh
Kept quiet on Baghdad to glorify Manchester
Favour to Vegas over Mogadishu

The issue seen here is their date proximities
The incidents mere days apart
But still the conflict goes further
As we unearth hashtags
To pomp and parade
No longer celeb-based but now stately placed as
Icons of the irony that
Fake computer prayer
Is used in the face of
Religion we fear
#pray for
The words so unsettling
For their presence brings
The silence of #ignore

Did you know
665 articles are written per death
In a Western strike
Just 60 if it happened elsewhere
…I didn't
Newspaper covers give victim profiles
From incidents
Deemed most significant
A gesture extended even

To the Western killers
Be it
Stephen's Paddock's music choice
Dylan Roof's softer side – and
Though we don't condone them
We don't quite other them
We keep them apart from the rage
We call terror
Where we can shout ISIS MUSLIM ISIS
Forget about the gun laws and rise of male supremacists
Cos - shhhh
No one likes a high and mighty moralist

Just give us our buzzword
Our latest trend, our greatest craze
Justify our fear
With a like on our status
Pat us on the back
For political au fait
Stay present in our wariness, for
When we place the blame elsewhere
It helps us
To feel
Safe

INTERLUDE 5

Well that was full on
I think I was wrong in choosing a move on
From the ease of hipsterdom
Life has got heavy
This obsessive animosity a far cry
From the lifestyle I led weeks earlier when the
Worst thing to fear was
My level of sunburn
Now the fervour is glaring
And really
All I want is to pull down the blindfold
Opt out from the crowd and keep myself solo
Focus on myself and my life and my goals
But there is no chance when the spotlight is on
How we each respond to political trends
And is it safe to go on holiday?
And isn't Europe in a state?
And maybe today's the day we reconsider immigration
And my god – the families of those Manchester children

And amidst it all
I'm feeling kind of lost, confused

by the
Misplaced anger
And displaced response
The inconsistency
Enough for me to know to dodge
This bandwagon of subjective compassion

Not entirely true

BERLIN

When my brothers called me from Berlin to say
A truck had driven in to the Christmas festivities
They were attending
I was paralysed
I was terrified
I watched
My Facebook timeline change before my eyes to
Flags, emojis and #Berlin
The world already in
Mourning for the city my brothers were still in
I tuned in to the livestreams
I followed every step of the unfolding action that said:

8:30 pm:
German media are reporting that the driver is on the run.
8:37pm:
Berlin police confirmed that nine people have been killed and many injured.
8:42pm:
The police also ask people to stay at home and not spread rumours.

The death toll was rising, social media was rioting
And despite my previous scorn
I entirely endorsed it because
I imagined my brothers statistics
With rational thought distant
I was full of hatred for whoever it was did this

But they were safe, they came home
And with time I was able to
Step back and reflect
Comprehend the experience as
The brush with disaster
We each meet so frequently, unknowingly
The speeding car, the faulty appliance
The drunk man looking for violence
Hindsight mindset quieted
And righted perspective, after all -
In the UK your chance of being killed in a terror incident
Sits at around one in 2.2 million, with
The US a hefty one in 5 million
Theirs was just bad luck
Met protective sibling love

Still I found myself question the extremity

Of responses from those who had no
Connection to the action
Those so quick to post a status, write a tweet
Profiles dripping in hashtags
Photos painted in slapdash
German flag brightness
Symbolic of what?
Offers of support? Declaring solidarity?
Because to me, something's hazy
When global tragedies have happened daily for centuries
Why this sudden attraction?
Why this assumption of blanket emotional grieving
Bereft of nuance through labelled reference to
The Muslims, the terrorists, ISIS, the West
As though
There must be a culprit, whatever the cost
The individual lost in the quest for binary justice
The crux in us claiming a nation as our own
To mourn for no apparent reason
It makes me wonder whether
Our hashtag prayers are saying
We stand with you, or
We stand against them
Makes me wonder

Who counts as you
And who counts as them

NICOLAS

Nicolas died in Somalia
When I met him we were both staying
In Gran Canaria
I told him he reminded me of my brother
Both fiercely determined and destined to be doctors
He said is that right
He said
Your brother
Must be smart, funny and handsome too then
I laughed and said yes

The bomb was so strong that most victims
        could not be identified
It took me 5 weeks to learn of his fate
Every day I saw papers detail
        the events of the shooting in Vegas
58 victims described and mourned
Yet just two weeks later
Over 300 Somalians ignored
I learned more news of strangers
Than the boy I'd learned to surf with

As though covering his life had not been deemed worth it

I looked at Nicolas and saw my brother
Others looked at him
And saw the third world urchins
The BBC leak through Comic Relief sob reels
We're taught they're used to extremities
So we could not assimilate
He was too much other
He must not have suffered
He was too much other

OTHER

Now remember:
Different - it sells
Different is sexy
Different is celebrated
Different is business

Other is not
Other is the flip side of different

Where
Different is quirky
Other is irregular
Where
Different is novel
Other is undesired
Where
Different is thrilling
Other is threatening
Where
Different is us
Other is them

Other emerged surreptitiously
One minute there was natural difference
Now active disinterest
It all happened so quick

Other is a thing undefinable
Is kind of confusing
Is can't quite put my finger on it
But I don't quite like it
Other is unknown
Other is maybe not to be trusted
(Or could it be that
Other is media-constructed
Is government-funded
Could just be a scapegoat
To accommodate blame shifts)
But in this day and age
Who's taking chances?

So let's have
Other all encompassing
For the sake of convenience
For the sake of safety
Other just wants to make sure so

Other becomes any other
Becomes refugee

Become immigrant, migrant, asylum seeker,
                                        eastern, foreigner
Other becomes colour
Other becomes darker
Other becomes definite terrorist

Other spreads and it shrinks
Is all and is local
Other becomes that homeless fellow
That Big Issue seller
That shopkeeper whose lived here 40 years
But you've never quite looked at him
        as you're looking at him now
And with all that's going on, well, you can't be too careful!

Where
Different is quirky
Other is irregular
Where
Different is novel
Other is undesired

Where
Different is thrilling
Other is threatening
Where
Different is us
Other is them

I look back and cringe at the way
I exploited my difference

INTERLUDE 6

We've turned a safe bunch, haven't we?

So much so one would believe
That with our fear of the unknown
Permeating our thinking
We would turn insular
Would not add kindle to
What's keeping us insecure
We would not risk all
That lies out there
We'd reject the foreign
Stay with the familiar
Right?

Not entirely true

IRONY

£20 RYANAIR RETURN TO LANZAROTE
GAP YEAR SPENT GETTING SMASHED WITH AUSSIES
HEN DO TO ZANTE
TATTOO IN SANSKRIT
WHITE PERSON DREADS BECAUSE SHAKIRA ROCKED IT

Yet we want to preserve our Britishness

PAKISTANI SALONS COS THEIR BROWS ARE ON FLEEK
£10 ON HALLOUMI COS THE BEST FOOD IS GREEK
3AM CURRIES
TAJ MAHAL SELFIES
BUT WE WILL NOT LET THEM COME INTO OUR COUNTRY

Do you see the irony?

That we embrace the conveyor belt of foreign experience,
                                                              yet maintain
The illusion we're somehow exempt from the
Rules and restrictions we impose on Others
When it comes to us

The options are limitless
With globe-trotting impetus
We form us a pick 'n mix
Of gap years, hen dos, sabbaticals, Erasmus
As westerners, borders don't seem to exist for us
We're expats, not immigrants
Migrate in our millions
Yet Britain helped only a trainload of Syrians

Do you see the irony?

That I was applauded for making my living
Performing on foreign streets
I was interviewed by easyJet
Praised for my initiative
Yet what I really did
Was compete with local artists
Take the lion's share of it
And feel that I deserved it
Because I was 'different'

Do you see the irony?

Of my indulgence in gluttonous

Exile

Meanwhile thousands upon thousands
Are ousted from their homelands
Just to be called intruder
With refuge refused
By those with the power to help them

Do you see the irony?

That we worry one dangerous person will come
So deny their entire nation
Yet our troops invade them
With weapons, agendas and alleged protection
And we still expect our vacations

Do you see the irony?
Do you see the irony?
I did not see the irony
More likely I ignored the irony

How our lives reek of privilege
We have not been taught limits when it comes to ownership
We know only to take
We do not think to give

We can work anywhere as au pair, barman, tour guide, teacher
Yet an unfamiliar accent sees us question their place here
How empathy deficient
What obstinate vision
If we go abroad to get wasted
Why can't people come here for safety?
The flaws on display are outrageous

We close our own eyes
We tie our own blindfolds
We choose to back down, to opt out
And for what?

DORIN

Dorin's son is so young, he doesn't remember life in Syria
To him, home is Glasgow
He doesn't recall his dad as a lawyer, dressed in suits
Instead, he knows only his Big Issue vest
Which he'll wear whenever he gets the chance
Dorin's son supports Celtic and asked his dad for a strip
So he could play games with the boys at school, now
Dorin doesn't have much money but he saved every penny
To purchase the shirt so his kid could fit in
Dorin was walking back from town
When a man saw him carrying the bag from the Celtic store
He pushed Dorin to the side of the road
Told him not to steal our culture
And in broad daylight
Beat him until his point had been made

Nobody stopped to help

Dorin was angrier at himself for getting blood on the shirt
And having to miss a week of work
Than he was at the man who attacked him

Dorin has been told he should be grateful for his place here
Whatever the cost

People make Glasgow, do they?

We close our own eyes
We tie our own blindfolds
We choose to back down, to opt out
And for what?

We must just be cold-hearted, compassionless robots

Part Three

INTERLUDE 7

I must be a cold-hearted compassionless robot
I must be a cold-hearted compassionless robot

Not entirely true?

As humans
Our very nature sees us programmed to nurture
To search for solution
To offer protection
Wherever we can and is relevant yet
I've seen the best minds of my generation
Look inwards not outwards
When faced with the option to help
So what's stopping us?
Something must be stopping us

Then it dawns that perhaps
Our flaw is not our kindness or lack thereof
But our mindless absorbing
Acceptance of that which we
See, which we
Hear, which we

Read
Our
Glue our eyes to every screen
Bow to social media preaching
Take the news as gospel
Way of being

Our placid surrender
To the sedative of the incessant detestable cesspool
That presents mere fragments of the larger truth
To see us generalise
To have us subjectively cry
To encourage that we pick and choose
To tell us there's nothing we can do
To stop any of it
And we trust implicitly
In all that this media utters

Even when it is not entirely true

NOT ENTIRELY TRUE

So when the media says let's only present some facts, we believe all we hear is entirely true. When the media fear mongers with its quick news, bad guys, and big headlines, we think they're entirely true. When the media focuses on terror terror terror to detract from our leaders' own behaviour, we think they're entirely true. When the media tells us they are impenetrable, better to fight the underdog instead ...

We think yes - that's entirely true

When the media sees we need someone to blame so they give us a scapegoat, we say that's entirely true, cos if we don't blame them then who? When the media knows if they oversaturate us with stories and horror and language, we'll surrender to distraction. So instead the media assures that if you put a hashtag on it, you've done your bit, it'll all be okay ...

That's just not true.

INTERLUDE 8

But we do it
Why do we do it?
Is it indicative of the millenial condition
That sees life confined to online significance
Or is it worse?
Are we callously surfaced flimsy beings
Abandoning action via hashtag hypocrisy
Or is the truth -
That in this OVERSATURATED WORLD
The chance to PACKAGE OUR SENTIMENT
Into a HASHTAG
To mark it as DONE
Allows us to FEEL WE'VE CONTRIBUTED
SOMETHING
To the world that MAKES US FEEL
UTTERLY HELPLESS

INTERLUDE 9

Well
That got a bit much, didn't it
Almost lost sight of it all for a minute there
If you don't mind -
I think I'll turn it down for a bit
And that's okay

HELEN AND AMAL II

Helen and Amal feed the birds in Queens Park every morning

I liked to chat with them, we shared travel stories

One day I saw that Amal was crying

An ISIS attack on London Bridge

Had left people dead

She was afraid of how people would see her

An incident 400 miles away

An incident of no relation to her

Left her afraid of how people would see her

Helen put her arm around Amal

It's okay, she said

Right now there's just us

And I see you for you

I see you

Okay? said Helen

Okay, said Amal

IT'S OKAY

It's okay to feel completely overwhelmed

It's okay to feel everything sometimes and nothing at others

It's okay to want to turn off from it all one day

Until the next when guilt grips and

You scream

Not in my name

And the conflict rips at you

It's okay

To want to hide from the news

Want to climb into bed

Want to drink to run to close your eyes

To feel like a tiny speck of nothing

Cos you're made to feel like a tiny speck of nothing

In the face of it all

It's okay

For what is people power if not the collective behaviour

Of a thousand specks of nothing

You are doing okay

You are doing okay

Just stay mindful

In a world constructed primarily from innocence
Retain perspective
In a world where you're handed the platform of privilege
Use it to reject the fallacies and retain perspective
In a world where Muslim civilians stood on streets blindfolded
Arms outstretched to welcome embrace or attack
                while guilty of nothing
Retain perspective
In a world where children had to protect
                their names by creating
Not My Islam
Retain perspective
In a world where people are forced to your shores
                seeking a hand, not bringing hostility
Retain perspective
In a world where the personal is political
It is inevitable that
Power lies in the individual
When you have been born with more power than many
There must be no question that you retain perspective

For there is no room left for botched excuses or hidden truths
When you retain perspective you reclaim direction
We are near the extent of pretending bewilderment

The time is imminent to
Think independent of influence
To see without blindfold hinderance
After all the answer's quite simple

View people as people

When you truly do so there's no space for ignorance
Intimidation or prejudice
When you view all people as people
Return to the basics, lead with the basics
This uncluttered vision
Will instigate change
And that
Is entirely true

SPECULATIVE BOOKS